AFFILIATE MARKETING INFLUENCE

THE ULTIMATE GUIDE TO LEARNING STEP-BY-STEP ABOUT BECOMING MORE INFLUENTIAL AT AFFILIATE MARKETING

Disclaimer

This e-book has been written for information purposes only. Every effort has been made to make this e-book as complete and accurate as possible.

However, there may be mistakes in typography or content. Also, this e-book provides information only up to the publishing date. Therefore, this e-book should be used as a guide - not as the ultimate source. The purpose of this e-book is to educate. The author and the publisher does not warrant that the information contained in this e-book is fully complete and shall not be responsible for any errors or omissions.

The author and publisher shall have neither liability nor responsibility to any person or entity with respect to any loss or damage caused or alleged to be caused directly or indirectly by this e-book.

AFFILIATE MARKETING INFLUENCE

Table of Contents

Introduction 8
    Affiliate Marketing: What Is It and How Can You Be Successful? 8
    Pick A Good Niche.. 8
    Design An Appealing Website 9
    Make Use Of Freebies... 9
    Learn To Target Your Traffic Back To Your Site 9
    Your Path To Affiliate Marketing Success.. 10

Chapter 1: What Can An Affiliate Marketer Expect Life To Be Like.. 13
    7 Tips To Be Successful In Affiliate Marketing 15

Chapter 2: Affiliate Marketing Tips To Help Your Campaign Succeed 18
    Pick A Product You Have Confidence In 19
    Don't Directly Sell The Product 19
    Key Tips To Create Success For Your Affiliate Marketing Program.......... 20
        Shorten Affiliate Links 20
        Write Reviews 20
        Promote Money-Making Products Only....................................... 20
    Ways To Successful Advertise Your Affiliate Marketing Campaign.......... 21
        Email Marketing 21
        Create a Tools Page 22
        Use Bonuses 22
        Use Banners 22

Chapter 3: Real Result Tips To Ensure Your Affiliate Marketing Campaign Is Successful 24
    You Must Have Patience 24

To Make Money, You Need To Spend Some 25
Start Monetizing Your Blog Right Away 25
Learn About Your Target Audience 25
Honesty Is Best For Selling Something 25
Effective Tips To Apply Toward Your Affiliate Marketing Campaign 26
Make A Positive First Impression 26
Promote Products You Own or Use 26
Effectively Promote The Product 26
Content Is First, Then Affiliate Links 27
Don't Promote Too Many Different Products 27

Chapter 4: What It Takes To Become A Successful Affiliate Marketer 29
Research, Research and More Research 29
Baby Steps 30
Learn About SEO and Other Tools 30
Be Passionate About Your Affiliate's Product 30
Learn About Your Target Audience 30
What Ads Will You Use? 31
What Tools Can You Use To Market Your Affiliated Product/Service 31
Videos 31
Written Content 31
Forums and Blogs 31

Chapter 5: What Kinds of Programs Sell Better In Affiliate Marketing 34
Why Is Conversion So Important? 35

Chapter 6: Should You Blog Or Not Blog Your Affiliate Product 38
Positive Aspects Of A Blog 39

Negative Aspects Of A Blog 39
Creating Your Affiliate Website and Earning Money From It 41

Chapter 7: Super Affiliates: Who Are They and What Is Their Life Like 44
What's A Typical Day Like For A Super Affiliate 46

Chapter 8: How To Use Search Engines To Generate Traffic For Your Affiliate Business 49
Key Tips To Remember When Using Linking Strategies 50

Chapter 9: What You Must Do To Increase Your Affiliate Program Earnings 53
Find A Good Product To Promote 54
Write Content To Give Away 54
Develop A Newsletter or E-Zine To Post Online 54
Submit Written Content To Article Directories 55
Include An Opt-In Option 55
Provide Bonuses 55
Ask For Higher Commissions 55
Some Helpful Tips To Keep In Mind 56

Chapter 10: How To Avoid Complaints Of Spam As An Affiliate Marketers 58
What Should You Be Mindful Of To Avoid The Spammer Designation? 59

Conclusion 61
What Are You Interested In? 61
Using Your Passion Isn't Always Best 62

INTRODUCTION

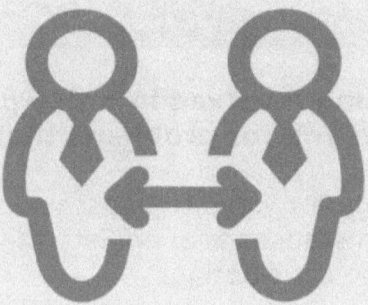

**AFFILIATE MARKETING
INFLUENCE**

Introduction

Are you tired of being involved in office politics or the boss constantly berating you for problems that are not your fault?

Have you been looking for ways to boost your household's income? Whatever your circumstances are, affiliate marketing is one potential journey you should be considering.

Affiliate Marketing: What Is It and How Can You Be Successful?

Affiliate marketing is a business opportunity that allows you to make a passive income by marketing company products. The income you make is through the commissions. Of course, for success to be had in this field, there are some important points for you to keep in mind:

Pick A Good Niche

When it comes to affiliate marketing, you need to pick an interesting niche or product. This little detail is a big one for your earnings. If there's a field you have a particular interest in, you can choose which affiliate program to get involved with. Create a list of things that interest you and look at the various programs to see what match them.

Design An Appealing Website

If you're going to be successful with affiliate marketing, you need to develop an eye-appealing website that's easy for your visitors to navigate and connects with them. The idea is¬ to convert these visitors into buyers or referrals. Make sure you have a well-designed landing page that includes a call-to-action (something that encourages the visitor to take the action you want them to).

Make Use Of Freebies

It's important to have helpful content to offer your visitors, as this translates to money for you. Everybody loves to get something for free. By offering freebies, you entice your visitors to become customers or referrers.

Learn To Target Your Traffic Back To Your Site

It doesn't matter how good your website looks or how useful a product is if your visitors can't find you. Consider techniques like SEO (search engine optimization) and link building to drive your target audience back to the site. Word of mouth and social networking are also helpful in spreading the word about the service/product you are offering.

There is a multitude of ways that you can use to entice people to visit your site:

- **Article Marketing** – this means writing material that you submit to directories that others pick up to publish.

- **Social Media Marketing** – this means using your social media accounts to inform people about the affiliate sites. You can also reach out to influencers and other contacts to spread word about what you're offering.

With the helpful tips above, failure as an affiliate marketer is less likely to happen.

Your Path To Affiliate Marketing Success

There are thousands of Internet entrepreneurs trying to make a name for themselves – to become a part of the affiliate marketing industry. With the boom in e-commerce and the Internet taking over the business world, choosing to become an affiliate marketer can be a lucrative option.

In order to be successful, however, you need to learn the basics of the business. What sacrifices are you going to be making to ensure your goals come to fruition? For you to be the best of the best, sacrifices are liable to be made.

Before joining a program, learn as much as you can about the company you will be representing. Thanks to the Internet, you can easily find out about a company. Stick with a company that has been in business for many years, as you can verify their claims a bit easier.

If the company is new, be sure the owner is credible.

As an affiliate marketer, it's always good to be wary. After all, you don't want to waste your time, money and other resources.

Most people are under the mistaken impression that affiliate marketing means not investing anything into the campaign. Wrong. You're free to join the program, but you still have to invest money to be successful. This money is usually tied to website promotion and advertising. Of course, if done successfully, you can get a return on the investment in time.

Affiliate marketing success takes time, dedication and hard work. The more effort and time you put into the business, the more successful you can be. The point is to always be willing to work hard and not bow out when times get tough. You will see earnings, but it takes time to see them like you want.

Come up with various techniques and strategies to make a big impact on your targeted audience. Be sure you create an engaging website and promote your products where your target audience is at. You'll have to advertise the product and engage with your audience. More of your time is spent on the program's initial months. However, as you establish a network, you'll see a lighter workload.

Yes, affiliate marketing can be tedious in the beginning. However, you have a large swath of support online, so make use of them when you have questions or concerns. And, know that you are not alone in this venture. There are hundreds of novice affiliate marketers in the same boat as you.

Most businesses and organizations have 24 hours a day, seven days a week customer support and support forums to assist affiliates with their questions and concerns. Many websites have articles, e-books, tips and tutorials that can help you become successful as an affiliate marketer.

Are you still interested in becoming an affiliate marketer?

CHAPTER 1:
WHAT CAN AN AFFILIATE MARKETER EXPECT LIFE TO BE LIKE

AFFILIATE MARKETING
INFLUENCE

Chapter 1: What Can An Affiliate Marketer Expect Life To Be Like

Thanks to the Internet, it's not as difficult to become and run an affiliate marketing business.

In the past, people had to use telephones and other forms of information to spread word about up and coming programs.

With this technology, and with the assumption that an affiliate stays at home to work, he/she could expect life to go a little like this:

• Wake up, power on the computer and have breakfast.

• Go back to the computer to see what new development has occurred in the network. The marketer may be concerned about the latest things going on with the network or looking over the statistics.

- They may redesign their website, as they know a well-thought-out and designed website will lead to an increase in signups and conversion rates.

- After they've done this, they'll submit the affiliate program to various directories, which are geared to attract the attention of people who may want to join the program.

- You start to track down the sales your affiliates are making. You may have emails and phone orders to track. What new clients are checking out the products? You need to write down contact information, as you never know when it'll be useful later on.

- You'll have to look through the various resources – button ads, banners, ads, sample recommendations, etc. A marketer knows that this helps with visibility and can all lead to sales.

- You'll have to answer emails from visitors. The sooner you do this, the better, as everybody wants to be heard. You'll have to pay attention to inquiries. Nobody likes being ignored, and people can be impatient. Answer their questions quickly and professionally.

- Log into a chatroom where you regularly interact with other affiliates using the program. You can discuss how best to promote products. Always be willing to learn from others, share your advice and provide support. You may have other people who want to join the program but need a little encouragement to do so.

- Find new methods to reaching out to your audience. In the past, you had ezines and newsletters, but newer techniques have come available. This information will be distributed to the affiliate's current and new customers.

- Bear in mind that these publications can help you learn about new products entering the market. The marketer may have a sale going on that customers want to learn about. They'll also have to keep up with the sales deadlines within these publications.

- Now, you'll need to give some appreciation to those people who have helped you become successful with their sales and promotions. Make sure to mention them and their sites as well as the process they used to make things work. This information should be published in a newsletter or on your social media site.

• You will also need to write our recommendations to people who want credible sources for promoted products. You can also make comments on how to be successful as an affiliate marketer on a website where people want to become one.   You kill two birds with one stone – you promote the product as the program it's in.

• Time has flown, and now it's time for bed.

Of course, the reality is that you won't get this all done in one day, but it provides you with an idea of what life is like for a typical affiliate marketer.

Do you smell success yet?

7 Tips To Be Successful In Affiliate Marketing

You may have made the decision to become an affiliate marketing, but what steps do you take next? The first thing you must understand is affiliate marketing will not make you rich overnight. It will take time to establish your stream of income, so make sure you're patient and stick to it. What are the most important tips to becoming successful with affiliate marketing?

Establish Relationships – When it comes to affiliate marketing, it boils down to one word: trust. You can have a friend recommend products to you, and you'll listen to what they have to say. However, a total stranger recommending products to you, you'll take with a grain of salt. You must establish trust with visitors to get them to listen to you.

Pick Products That Solve Problems – Many affiliate marketing programs can address a person's need for a problem. Invest in that program.

Focus On Bringing Traffic To Your Site – You want traffic coming to your website because that means you have the potential to turn them into customers. You'll need to work hard to get build up the traffic.

Promote Wisely – It will take time to promote your affiliate marketing products. No longer are the days of banner ads and paid ads. Today, you have to inform visitors about the good and bad aspects of the product. Inform them how it can help them and what they may not like about it.

Use Analytical Tools To See What's Working and What's Not – It's important to learn what is and isn't working for your business. You can't guess that an ad is working because it may not be. Rather than play the guessing game, use any of the vast array of analytical tools to find out what campaigns are working for you. This information will help you to get rid of campaigns that are failing and putting that money into something else that will work.

Reach Out To Experts – There are a copious number of affiliate networks. If you need help, sign up with one. They provide an array of support and services such as tools, strategies, support, development, etc. This information will help you to increase your campaign's revenue

Make Honest Assessment About Your Recommendations – Honesty can go a long way. Don't over embellish about a product because people can see through the lies and this can lead them to turn away from what you have to offer. If they can't trust you, they'll never do business with you. Make an honest assessment of the product you are advertising. Do not ever try to deceive your visitors.

With these helpful tips, you can reap the benefits that other affiliate marketers have long been enjoying.

CHAPTER 2:
AFFILIATE MARKETING TIPS TO HELP YOUR CAMPAIGN SUCCEED

AFFILIATE MARKETING
INFLUENCE

Chapter 2: Affiliate Marketing Tips To Help Your Campaign Succeed

Many people think of affiliate marketing as the boogeyman – something so scary that it's impossible to be successful.

For other people, it's about creating an ad, sitting back and watching the money rake in. What's affiliate marketing really?

It's the middle ground between the two thoughts!

If you're unfamiliar with affiliate marketing, here's what you should first understand about it – it's a way to produce income while you sell another's person product.

Several things can be done to ensure you're successful, but there are two key important affiliate marketing tips to keep in mind:

- Pick a product you have confidence in
- Don't directly sell the product

If you do this correctly, you can produce a reasonable income with affiliate marketing without having to need your own money to stock the products. While you don't need them for complete success, they do go a long, long way in helping you to achieve it.

Pick A Product You Have Confidence In

There are millions of products up for sale on the market, with many of them offering an affiliate program to get involved in. It's up to you to find a product that you feel confident in. Perhaps this is something you have used for yourself or that you've done a lot of research on before becoming an affiliate marketer for it. If you're going to sell the product to other people, you should have confidence in what you're selling.

Answer this question: is this product worth promoting – something other people should know about? If the answer is yes, then you should try being an affiliate marketer for it.

Don't Directly Sell The Product

Many affiliate marketers make the mistake of selling a product as if it's their own. Remember, it's not something you own or have control over. The idea is to promote the product using your own experience. Talk about the product in terms of "In my experience," "The product was useful to me in" or "I liked this product because" – something to this effect.

This lets people know that you are not the true owner of the product and establishes a person's trust in you. If they see you as helpful rather than trying to sell something, they're bound to give you their trust. There's no pressure to buy, which increases the chance they'll buy.

The best way to make a good income from affiliate marketing is to be honest. People are tired of the lies and gimmicks people use to make money, especially on inferior or less than useful products. If you can offer a high-quality affiliate marketing product – something that people can use – you'll sell the product faster and earn a good living through this kind of program.

Key Tips To Create Success For Your Affiliate Marketing Program

You can enjoy a steady stream of income with an affiliate marketing program, but it must be done correctly to ensure this happens. If done incorrectly, you could be left wondering what you forgot to do. Consider the following tips below to help you kick off a successful affiliate marketing campaign:

Shorten Affiliate Links

You want to get rid of the ugly affiliate links, which can be done with a link cloaker tool. This will shorten the affiliate links, making them better to look at. It will also help boost your click-through rate.

For example, a Clickbank.com affiliate program may have a link like http://AFFILIATE.VENDOR.hop.clickbank.net.

However, if you were to use a link cloaker program, you could shorten it to http://yourdomain.com/this-product.

Write Reviews

Written reviews do wonders for affiliate marketing programs. A review talks about a product, letting people know what the pros and cons are of the products, so readers are better informed about it. You could also compare a similar product to the one you are marketing.

Come up with a category only for the reviews, making it visible to visitors. Consider adding a rating plugin for the reviewed products to be rated. The stars will indicate how people feel about the quality. The more positive reviews you have, the higher the chance for more sales.

Promote Money-Making Products Only

There are millions of products on the market that you can choose from, but you need to find products that will garner you a good commission. Steer clear of programs that don't appear to be doing well. Should you avoid cheap ticket items? Not at all. After all, a $20 product could have a 20 percent commission while a $100 product has a 10 percent commission. It's easier to sell people on the cheap products. Which one would be better for your income?

Make sure you choose the program wisely.

The idea is to build a lucrative stream of income, which means you need to test products out to see how well they're doing. There may be times that you think a product will do well and doesn't. But, the only way to know for sure is to test, test and do it all over again.

There you go – three useful tips to ensure your affiliate marketing program is a success.

Ways To Successful Advertise Your Affiliate Marketing Campaign

You already know that affiliate marketing can generate a good income for your household. But, you can't just choose an affiliate and start selling. You have to advertise the product you're an affiliate marketer for. How do you do this?

Email Marketing

Most people don't realize it just yet, but email marketing is the gift that keeps on giving. But, in order for success to be had with email marketing, you need to have a list of subscribers to send emails to. You can do this by offering an opt-in option for your blog or website. Entice people to sign up, offering them a free e-book, monthly newsletter, percentage off coupons, etc.

You want them to provide you with their email address. As the list grows, you have more prospective customers to entice with your emails. Don't send them too many emails though, as this can lead to their unsubscribing. You also don't want to promote your product in every single email you send them, as it will also have negative consequences.

The idea is to build a rapport with them and subtly encourage them to purchase the product.

Create a Tools Page

A tools page is where you list the tools used (or the products/services you've experienced firsthand). With this page, your visitors can quickly see what you have on hand, without it looking like a shopping page. You list the item using a link and have a short review about it.

Use Bonuses

If you really want to gain a person's business, consider giving them the affiliate offer along with another bonus item if they purchase. This could be a discount of some sort or another product you don't mind giving away. Consider thinking outside the box to entice your visitors to become customers. With handsome commission payouts, you have some wiggle room to offer such benefits to your visitors (and yourself).

Use Banners

Add banners to your blog or website, putting them in the header, footer, sidebar or content. Affiliate products often have two banner ads that let you choose a promote that you want to promote. Banners see the highest click-through rates for any ads or promotion created.

CHAPTER 3:
REAL RESULT TIPS TO ENSURE YOUR AFFILIATE MARKETING CAMPAIGN IS SUCCESSFUL

AFFILIATE MARKETING
INFLUENCE

Chapter 3: Real Result Tips To Ensure Your Affiliate Marketing Campaign Is Successful

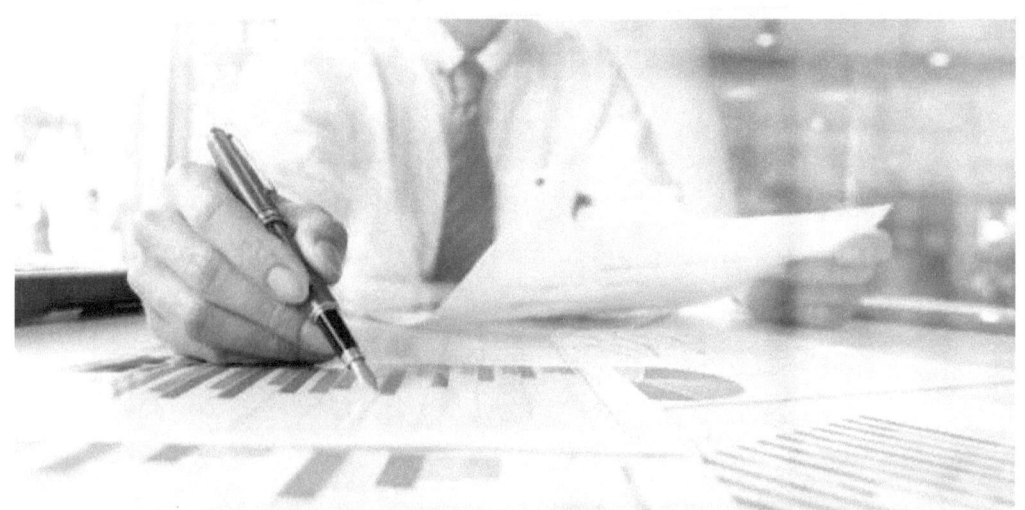

People who become affiliate marketers do it to make money. While a little money is good, a lot of money is better.

The idea is to develop a residual stream of income. With some helpful tips, you can make this happen. Of course, you need first to research the affiliate program to see if something is worthwhile.

You Must Have Patience

The biggest reason website owners and bloggers fail at affiliate marketing is their lack of patience. They make little money in the beginning, giving up the chance of earning more. It's not easy to make money from an affiliate marketing program, but with some patience, you do make it. Don't think of affiliate marketing as a way to get rich quick. That doesn't happen. It's going to take both patience and time to ensure it happens.

To Make Money, You Need To Spend Some

If you're going to make any money, you need to spend some of it. You must spend money to produce a steady flow of income. Purchase the products you want to market to others. This will help you to learn about them. What do you like? What do you not like?

If you're going to make recommendations, it's best to it based experiences you've had. If you've not done your homework on the product or used it yourself, you won't be able to make money promoting it.

There's no reason to spend a copious amount of money on the product; you do need to spend some to learn about it.

Start Monetizing Your Blog Right Away

There's no reason you have to wait to monetize your blog. This is a huge mistake novice affiliate marketer make. You can begin selling products/services immediately. You should always get to learn about the product so that you can become passionate about it. This passion will show through in how you market to your target audience.

Learn About Your Target Audience

When you start marketing your product, it's best to know who you'll be marketing. Who are they? Where do they live? What kind of income do they have? What products are they often buying? Knowing your readers and audience allows you to pick a product that you can advertise to and make money on.

Honesty Is Best For Selling Something

When you're honest about something, you build trust and rapport with your target audience. Make sure that you answer all questions people have about the product as honestly as you can. Let them know what you really think of a product – it's good and bad sides. Everybody knows that all products have a flaw, so don't try claiming that the product is perfect. No one is going to believe that.

Effective Tips To Apply Toward Your Affiliate Marketing Campaign

Affiliate marketing provides you with the chance to make passive income. To make this happen, however, you know what has worked previously and led to success for many established affiliate marketers. What tips should you apply to your own affiliate marketing campaign?

Make A Positive First Impression

You may have heard it before, but it should be stated again – first impressions are everything. It doesn't matter if you're trying to sell something or you're meeting someone for the first time. What happens the first time you meet someone will create an impression.

Your visitors are going to get an impression of your website the first time they visit it. How your website is set up will create a tone that resonates with them. Are they going to stay on the site and look around, buying something in the meantime? Or, are they going to leave because it didn't feel welcoming enough?

Your landing page must be appealing and friendly – to ensure visitors feel like they're more than just a sale.

Promote Products You Own or Use

When selling a product, it's a good idea to know about the product you are trying to market. Consider buying it for yourself to see if it's worth the hype. If not, then you shouldn't be trying to sell your visitors on it. This kind of action can lead to negative consequences such as a bad reputation.

Effectively Promote The Product

You may put up a banner ad or an affiliate graphic ad, but if you don't provide a description of what you're trying to selling, you're not going to sell it. It cannot be stressed enough how much you should know about a product to effectively promote it to others. Craft a through, but a creative piece of content that lets visitors know what you know about the product and why they would benefit from using it as well.

By sharing what you have learned, it encourages them to purchase the product for themselves.

Content Is First, Then Affiliate Links

Too often, people make the mistake of focusing on links and not content. Don't do this. You should focus more on website content then deal with affiliate links. The content you develop needs to be high-quality material with no intention of an affiliate link. Give your visitors something valuable.

Don't Promote Too Many Different Products

There are many types of products you can be marketing for sale, which may be tempting for you to promote the different ones. Don't do this if you want to be a success story. Choose one or two products that are identical and promote them. This will help boost your chances for success.

Why?

If you promote multiple products, your visitors are going to be skeptical that you've tried all and can provide them with an adequate assessment of the product. If you recommend Business A, then B and C, how do you establish a rapport and trust with the visitor?

CHAPTER 4:
WHAT IT TAKES TO BECOME A SUCCESSFUL AFFILIATE MARKETER

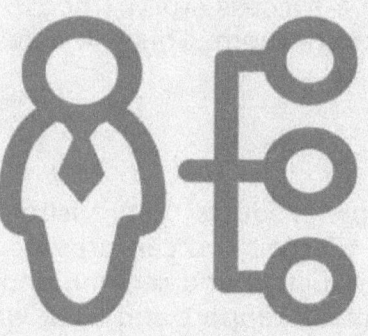

AFFILIATE MARKETING
INFLUENCE

Chapter 4: What It Takes To Become A Successful Affiliate Marketer

When you decide to earn an extra income from affiliate marketing, you want to ensure your success. How do you do this though?

What tips will help you to earn the passive income that affiliate marketing campaigns can bring?

Research, Research and More Research

You can't just post an affiliate's ad on your website and hope it brings in money. No, it doesn't work like that. For you to make money from an affiliate marketing campaign, you need to do some research on the product and its related industry. What kinds of opportunities does it have? Are there possible risks to using it?

You should find out what trends are current and how the product fits into those trends. Look at the various ways in which to advertise these products – social media, PPC, paid ads, etc.

Baby Steps

Before you jump into the fire, it's best to stay out of the frying pan. Learn how things work before you make the big decisions.

Get involved with an affiliate program that has meaning for you. Consider an automated ad code, which will allow the network manager to access it. Update the ads regularly, especially for special occasions such as Christmas, Labor Day, Valentine's Day, Easter, etc.

Learn About SEO and Other Tools

It's important if you plan to be found by your audience, to use SEO (search engine optimization) and tools that relate to it. Learn what keywords are and how they work. What tools will help you to be found by your audience and get them to purchase your product?

Be Passionate About Your Affiliate's Product

Your passion for an affiliate's product can do wonders in how you market it. If you can't get passionate about a product, then it's not the right affiliate product to get involved in. Look at the various products/services to find one that clearly resonates with you. Why do you like the product so much? Have you used it?

Share the passion you have by producing content that shows it. This will help to sell the product faster and lead to higher sales.

Learn About Your Target Audience

Success is only had when you know who your target audience of the product is. What do your prospective customers have in common with each other? Will this profile align with the product you're going to offer? If the answer is no, then you need to consider another product to market or come up with another customer profile.

What Ads Will You Use?

Once you learn who your target audience is and the product you'll be marketing, it's time to determine what kinds of ads you'll be using to market toward your audience. Will you produce a banner ad that encourages your visitors to click on it? Will they need to watch a video that encourages them to take action?

Whatever kind of ad you decide to use, you must add a call-to-action with it. You want your visitors to convert to buyers, and a call-to-action can make that happen.

What Tools Can You Use To Market Your Affiliated Product/Service

There are several ways you can be a successful affiliate marketer, but the biggest way is to show visitors how the product is used and how it benefits them. Nothing is better than getting your stamp of approval and showing visitors how to use the product.

Videos

Now, you may be wondering how you can show visitors the way to use the product you're trying to market. The simplest way to show your target audience is to create videos of you using the product. Post the video on your blog or YouTube. YouTube is great for "how to" videos. Come up with an interesting but honest video. Your video should be no more than four minutes long, as anything longer.

Written Content

You can also develop articles, reports and e-books to talk about the product and how it's used. Use this method to discuss the positive and negative aspects being honest about them. You want your visitors to know what you actually think of the product. This method, however, requires that you've tried the product.

Forums and Blogs

Make posts about the product, talking about how you found it, why you bought it and the way you used it. Did it solve your problem? Provide this information to your visitors. The more visitors that see these posts, the higher the probability of seeing sales.

Podcasts are another way to promote products and reach a new audience.

Your goal is to plant a seed of curiosity and foster it so that you can win your target market over. Let visitors know what you're offering, telling them how it will help them and any negative points to them. Create new content regularly to foster that connection and promote niche products.

Remember, success can be had, but only if you do your due diligence. This means doing your homework to find a product that's worth your time to invest in. What kind of product has a solid reputation? What product is high in quality? Does the affiliate marketing program offer a competitive commission compared to its competitors?

Don't forgo higher priced items because they are higher in price. Often times, these will sell better when marketed correctly. If you have a product that fits the niche you're in and you come up with a powerful marketing campaign, you can earn be profitable as an affiliate marketer.

CHAPTER 5:
WHAT KINDS OF PROGRAMS SELL BETTER IN AFFILIATE MARKETING

AFFILIATE MARKETING
INFLUENCE

Chapter 5: What Kinds of Programs Sell Better In Affiliate Marketing

When it comes to investing in a profitable affiliate marketing program, you need to look at the statistics of it. Of course, the reality is that what works for one person may not work for another.

Your visitors are the real indicator if a product will or will not be a profitable marketing venture for you. This means learning about your buyers and using techniques that help with your marketing and SEO efforts.

Did you know that there are two kinds of buyers?

- Buyers constantly doing research on products
- Buyers who think they need a product to solve an issue they have

Are there other kinds of buyers on the market? Sure are, but these folks are not real buyers that are ready to spend money. This is fluff traffic, which looks good on your analytics but not for your bottom line. You don't want to waste your time and energy on these so-called buyers.

This is when you need to do some keyword research. After all, effective keyword research targets people who are interested in buying, not those looking to possibly buy. You'll learn about the difference in another chapter.

It appears that the topic of niche selection has gone astray. Not to worry, as it all interweaves. In order to pick a niche, you need to understand how niches work. You have to know what programs will make you money using the above marketing tools.

Once you've got your niche set aside, you can create your business. Thus, you can develop a plan of action that lets you get involved with the action.

Why Is Conversion So Important?

Affiliates are curious about why conversions are so important? When all is said and done at the end of the day, conversion is the only thing that matters. Why? If your website visitors don't become buyers, you don't make money. It's plainly simple. Conversion is what leads to money.

Conversion is about what a large swath of people will do on the website or as a whole. You can't expect that all visitors will become buyers (though it would be nice if that happened). However, it is important to understand that what you're doing it working to garner your visitors' attention.

Conversions are about three things:

- Sales
- Statistics
- Rates

However, there are no actual rules you can apply. Rules differ for every product you market, as they have their own needs.

What you need to focus on is to boost your site's profitability – done by changing, testing and tweaking content until it produces the most amount of sales you've seen. There are several ways in which this can be done. There may be a lot of trial and error here. After all, the goal is to convert visitors into buyers, and you won't know what works without testing out your ideas.

So, as you see, conversions are important because they lead to sales.

CHAPTER 6:
SHOULD YOU BLOG OR NOT BLOG YOUR AFFILIATE PRODUCT

Chapter 6: Should You Blog Or Not Blog Your Affiliate Product

Blogosphere... it is the place where anybody can use a template or create a website and update it with content that people may consider useful or with information about their daily routine.

A blog is an extremely powerful tool that both website owners and businesses can use regularly. Think of it as a personal diary for anyone to check out.

The blogosphere includes newbies and experts as well as people who believe they're an expert but still a newbie. It's an amalgamation of people who make up the community, which has no boundaries to it.

Thus, a blog, which is the quickest and simplest way to promote products and earn an income, can make or break your affiliate program. What are blogs really all they've been hyped to be?

Positive Aspects Of A Blog

- You can easily start one.

- It doesn't cost a lot to get one going.

- You can upload valuable information for your visitors to read.

- You can use the various community tools at your disposal – commenting, virtual conversations, etc.

- You can foster a long-term relationship with readers that will lead to sales.

- You can feature your products on the blog.

- It's the easiest way for content to be updated so search engines can find it.

As you see, there are a plethora of benefits and blogging can be beneficial, but it must be done correctly in order for you see the return on investment when promoting your affiliate products.

Blogs are many things, and some of its qualities don't always fit into what an affiliate website is designed for.   Of course, before you decide to create a blog, you need to consider what the negative aspects are.

Negative Aspects Of A Blog

The factors that make blogging a good choice to do affiliate promotions are the same factors that, when done incorrectly, can hinder the affiliate's ultimate goal.

• The blogosphere is crowded, which means it's already loaded with an array of content. How is your blog going to stand out to get found? You can be the most dedicated and best blogger out there, but it will still take you years to establish a strong following. A blog will not give you immediate traffic.

• The community feature of blogging is wonderful, but it can lead to a free-for-all where comments others make can hurt you. How valuable is the commenting feature to your affiliate marketing program? This will depend a lot on your product offerings.

• If you offer various products, customers could come back to you or ask for an upgrade, which makes staying in touch with them a wonderful thing. However, a one-time-only buy means you don't have a good return on investment in your blog.

• Updated content is necessary for blogging. You can make a quick post on a daily basis, which both your followers and search engines want. However, the downfall is how often can you regurgitate the same thing about a product in a new way? Are the products going to be noted on the blog? What happens when your topics are all dried up? Your readers and the search engines will be waiting for new material, and you'll have nothing to give to them.

• You can easily start a blog and maintain it for several months, but if you're going to make real money, you need to come up with a long-term strategy to make it happen. While a blog can be a long-term project, you must say something new for it to live a long time.

• You also need to worry about featuring multiple products at one time. If you decide to invest your time and efforts into more than two products, you take the focus away from any particular one. This also confuses readers. You don't provide your readers with a simple answer to their problems.

• You're also limited in terms of structure for your blog. Unless you're constructing your own (it can be done but is difficult), chances are you will be using a template. Templates don't provide a lot of flexibility. You have the basic structure, and adding features and buttons where you want is difficult to do. Also, be mindful that your design and structure will be impacted by the number of postings you make as well as their length.

Should you consider a blog for your affiliate product? That's really up to you to decide, and it can be a very useful tool for marketing an affiliate product.

Creating Your Affiliate Website and Earning Money From It

The easiest part of your gig will be attaining affiliate links; it's the hosting part you'll need to contend with. Where will you host these links so that visitors become buyers? This will take some doing. You must come up with a place that people will find you, where they come looking for help or information and where they'll go through the buying process.

Difficult to do, but doable.

Before doing a single thing, you must come up with a strategy. Devise a plan that provides you with all the tools you need to sell.

There's no reason to get too involved about where to attain a website; you can easily find out this information for yourself. Of course, the most popular names are HostGator and GoDaddy, but there are a copious number of hosts and site-building templates available for people to use. A person can use the one their ISP gives them for free or be their own host.

The point you must remember is that anybody has the ability to develop a functional website, which brings in traffic.

The focus, however, should be more on the website's structure.

For example, if you're promoting multiple products, and want to make money like the experts, you need to provide each product with its own site. That means dedicating your time between two or more sites. The sites don't need to be big – a few pages in all (10 to 20 pages), depending on how many products you're selling.

However, you must include all the elements search engines are looking for. Do this, and this can lead to visitors and targeted traffic that may or may not convert to buyers.

As you establish yourself, you'll want to design a centralized website that directs visitors to the smaller websites that focus on a particular product. This website is used to clean up the non-targeted traffic due to the keywords used. These people are not always in "buy now" mode. Many times, they are in the "looking around now, buy later" mode.

While this is important, it can be addressed later. Your main focus should be building the individual sites and making money.

At the beginning of it all, your strategy will come to something similar:

- Target keywords, market and audience
- Pick certain affiliate products to promote
- Create a website around those particular groups of products
- Develop individualized websites for each product
- Design a master website that will target traffic and links them to the individualized products

Need some help visualizing this all? Here's a good example of this plan:

You're selling products related to fitness such as bodybuilding supplements, workout routines, workout equipment, etc. People who want muscle-building supplements don't care about the workout routines or equipment. Even if you put up ads, you don't come across as an authority on the subject.

Thus, you break them down into groups and market several of them together with their own website. Rather than one catch-all for the fitness-related material, you have a dedicated website for your visitors to check out and purchase from you. So, you have the following setup:

- 10 to 20-page website on bodybuilding supplements
- 10 to 20-page website for workout equipment

The sites provide your buyers what they're looking for, not what they don't need. Once these sites have taken off, you can create a main store that includes categories that direct back to the dedicated sites.

It's a structure set up that expert affiliates use to make their money.

CHAPTER 7:
SUPER AFFILIATES: WHO ARE THEY AND WHAT IS THEIR LIFE LIKE

AFFILIATE MARKETING
INFLUENCE

Chapter 7: Super Affiliates: Who Are They and What Is Their Life Like

How does an affiliate become a super affiliate? This is a person that succeeds in capitalizing on their income along with their advertisers for a certain period of time.

This person brings in a lot of traffic to their sites, surpassing all their competitors.

Well-known advertisers are always on the lookout for super affiliates. Advertisers know super affiliates can lead to a higher return on investment for marketing campaigns. There are certain attributes a super affiliate marketer will have that other affiliates will try and mimic to reach this highly-coveted status. What are some of these traits that you can try attaining for yourself?

They've researched and included important aspects of SEO and SEM (search engine optimization and search engine marketing) into their affiliate marketing campaign.

They've created at least one website (if not more). The websites are professionally-designed and engage with visitors without intrusive graphics that force them to click on banners or links to their affiliate's products.

They've optimized keyword searches to determine what the right keyword is to attain the attention of their targeted traffic to their websites.

They've come up with valuable content that blends in perfectly with their affiliate website. The content is fresh and informative about their promoted product.

They use text link ads in the HTML links to boost traffic going to the affiliate website.

They use a monitoring system that lets them see how their website is doing regarding ranking on the different search engines.

They'll use the Trellian search term to find particular keyword phrases that will help them to boost the amount of traffic going to their affiliate website.

They use link submissions and exchanges to increase the visibility of their web pages, which can lead to more site visitors.

They use various Internet business promotion tools to boost SEO of their website, which can help improve their search engine rankings.

They make use of W3C Certification to make sure the affiliate website is HTML compliant; thus, avoiding the possibility of being blocked by the different software programs that were created to restrict access to dangerous or fake websites.

The reality about super affiliates is that they work hard all the time, and they are extremely smart about the Internet – learning everything they can about it. This knowledge enables them to use every feature of digital marketing, SEO and SEM to get the most from their promotions. Most advertisers would rather work with super affiliates to get the most return on investment.

Why?

They know super affiliates get a higher click-through rate that leads to conversions than a novice affiliates.

What's A Typical Day Like For A Super Affiliate

Although the status of a Super Affiliate is one people want, it comes with enormous responsibilities. What could life be like if you become a super affiliate?

The first thing to contend with is turning on your computer so that it can boot up while you get breakfast. As you know, breakfast is regarded as the most important meal of the day. It helps the brain to function and gets the body moving.

After you eat, you can go back to the computer and look at what, if any, new developments have taken place. You may find out that you need to learn something new to stay ahead of your competition. You also need to look at your statistics. What's going on with your website? How well or poorly is it performing?

Your day's agenda focuses on redesigning the site. A super affiliate knows that a well-thought-out design that looks professional will lead to new visitors and higher conversion rates. The redesign has to be quick but professional.

You also need to look for sales figures and found some contact information.

So much as already been done, which means you can take a break from the computer and do something else for a short time.

You come back only to find that you have new banners and ads to contend with. As a super affiliate, you can use them when making recommendations. This lets you stay visible to the public, and eventually lead to more sales.

It's time for you to focus on visitors' email messages. You don't want to respond to them as they come in but in a timely fashion will do. You don't want them waiting long because this could make them think you don't care about them and their concerns. Keep your replies back as professional as you can. Use a friendly tone when writing back.

Review the social media sites to see what's going on and do a quick promotion on them.

You may need to contend with the e-zines and newsletters from the other day. Since things can change quickly in the market, you need to stay on top of what's going on. Look at the status and write down when the next publication's deadlines and promos are.

You get another email, but this time, it comes from a satisfied customer, which is something you can add to your next newsletter. Why not show people an example of how well your affiliate product is helping people, right?

Now, it's time to step away from the computer. A super affiliate has gotten a lot done in their day including answering questions from a novice affiliate who's trying to make a new for him/herself.

This is what success looks like for a super affiliate.

CHAPTER 8:
HOW TO USE SEARCH ENGINES TO GENERATE TRAFFIC FOR YOUR AFFILIATE BUSINESS

AFFILIATE MARKETING
INFLUENCE

Chapter 8: How To Use Search Engines To Generate Traffic For Your Affiliate Business

There's no denying the reality: Search engine traffic is a huge cornerstone of your business.

After all, without search engines, you could have no traffic to your website. And, the traffic you do get may not be enough to survive the market.

At least 90 percent of the traffic on your website is the result of search engines – mainly from the well-known sites like Yahoo, Google, Bing and MSN. These search engines can bring you thousands of visitors looking for the product and information you provide. Of course, search engines are not the only way you'll get traffic.

You also have the following methods:

- Links from articles and other websites
- Traditional marketing links and addresses

- Word of mouth

However, if you were to combine the traffic amount, this just translates to 10 percent of your visitor traffic. While 10 percent is nothing to sneeze or laugh at, your best bet (your focus) needs to be on search engine traffic.

When you put forth the effort to optimize your site, it leads to more links and exposure that allows your website to be found through the other methods. Thus, search engine marketing is essential for a business to thrive.

On top of that, search engine traffic is regarded as organic, which means it comes from actual human beings that are actively looking for a product/service that you have to offer. They look for these things to serve a purpose.

They may need to buy something, learn about something new, solve a problem, conduct a business promotion or whatever. The commonality is that that actual human beings are looking for somebody like you.

Link clicks or typing in your web address from a business card doesn't mean an active buyer. It just means a person is curious about who you are. People who use a search engine are using it for a reason – for a particular goal. Even if that goal for them wasn't to buy something, you could convince them that you have what they need and convert them to a buyer.

Key Tips To Remember When Using Linking Strategies

It's important, when using linking strategies, that you do it legally. In your research for linking strategies, you will come across an array of theories. For you, you have to be mindful of ones that could be problematic.

There are five key points to bear in mind if you decide to implement a linking strategy:

• Look over the links you're considering for other websites. It's not about quantity but quality when promoting your website. You want your page to rank well, but having large numbers of bad links is not a good thing. Focus on good quality links. You want these links to be valuable to your visitors as it speaks volumes about you and your site.

• Look at the various kinds of linking strategies to ensure they adhere to the search engines rules and guidelines. How effective as these linking strategies for your website? Are they increasing its visibility?

• Steer clear of programs that claim to provide you with a lot of links at one time. Most of these programs are linking schemes and will result in affecting your search engine page ranking negatively.

• Be wary of offers that promise you incoming links from high page ranking sites, as this is against the search engines' rules. If you've caught paying for links, your website could be banned from participating in them.

• Don't use automated linking programs to produce outbound links. These kinds of software keep the other site from getting the deserved credit for an incoming link. You can find out this information by hovering the cursor over the link.

At the bottom of your screen, you should see a status bar. If you notice the link is theirs, it's a good link. If the URL is longer, you don't get the benefit by the site you link to.

Website links will affect the value of your listing in the search engines. For that reasons, you want to learn how to do an effective linking strategy by looking for information on how to do this correctly. Do a search using any search engine, as they offer a plethora of information that will help you avoid possible problems when linking one site to your own.

CHAPTER 9:
WHAT YOU MUST DO TO INCREASE YOUR AFFILIATE PROGRAM EARNINGS

**AFFILIATE MARKETING
INFLUENCE**

Chapter 9: What You Must Do To Increase Your Affiliate Program Earnings

Most people who've contemplated beginning an online business have no idea where to begin. They may have signed up for an affiliate program and created a website to earn a little extra income.

However, they haven't succeeded in making this happen for them.

However, by now, you should have a good idea of how the affiliate marketing program works. You've taken the right steps to learn about the affiliate marketing program. You've done your homework, set up your page and things appear to be going smoothly. Of course, making money is nice but what if you could make even more money than you currently are. Would it not be nice to wake up one morning to see your commission's numbers have increased from the day before?

How can you make that happen for you?

Find A Good Product To Promote

Choose a product or program that will lead to higher profit margins in a short period of time. What should you consider when choosing a product or program?

Look for ones that offer a lavish commission structure – something that ties into what your target audience would be interested in. There are many kinds of affiliate programs to choose from, which means you can afford to be picky. Research the different programs before making your decision. You also want an affiliate program that pays you in a timely manner –not months from when you earn the income.

The idea to earn a good amount of money that makes it worth the effort and time you put into it. If you make a little money, that's good. But, you want a program that provides compensation for all your hard work.

Write Content To Give Away

Another way to earn more money is to develop free reports or a short e-book that visitors can download. The report and e-book can tie in with your promoted product, or it can provide information people may find relevant to their lives.

If you have competition (and the chances are high that you do), you need to find information that your competitors don't have just yet. You need to set yourself apart from them, which helps to boost your credibility and authority with your target audience.

Develop A Newsletter or E-Zine To Post Online

Another way to establish some connection with your visitors is to create a newsletter or set up an e-zine for them to visit and read. You can use the page to recommend products you're an affiliate marketer for. By establishing a rapport with the readers, you could influence their decision to purchase the product.

Submit Written Content To Article Directories

Again, content is king, and you can submit your articles about affiliate products to article directories. However, add a link that goes back to your site where the traffic will be directed so they can purchase the products you are promoting. Without this link, visitors never see the website and never see the product you are offering (from you anyway).

Include An Opt-In Option

In order to send emails to your audience about free updates on promoted products or programs, you need email addresses. You can collect this contact information by including an opt-in space for your visitors to sign-up. This will enable you to stay in contact with them; great when you have something special to offer them.

With regular emails, you remind them that you're still there for their needs.

Make sure that you use an autoresponder to send these emails to your audience. You can set it up so that you can deliver content as many times as you want in a day, week or month without having to contend with it yourself manually.

Provide Bonuses

You can offer your visitors bonuses that don't even relate to the promoted product. With many affiliates promoting the same service/product, you have to stand out to your target audience. Why should a new audience member purchase from you and not your competitor? Your established audience already know what you have to offer. But, you need to lay it on thick for the newbies. Give them some a little extra for their money. You want them to stay with you.

Ask For Higher Commissions

Granted, this will only work if you've been with a merchant for some time, making him/her some money through your campaigns. Ask the merchant if they will consider granting you a higher percentage of the commission. Do some negotiations here. Don't go in headstrong with your mind set on a particular commission percentage, as you're bound to walk away a loser.

Instead, be flexible. Ask the merchant the commission you'd like to have. If they're smart (and most are), they'll likely see you as an asset and agree to your rate. If they feel it's too high but that you deserve more, they'll counter with their own.

The keyword to remember is to be reasonable with your suggested percentage. You can't expect them to give you 75 percent commission earnings. That's liable not to happen. However, they are likely to give you an increase of some sort.

By employing the seven tips listed above, you can see your commission's checks increase in value. What are you waiting for?

Some Helpful Tips To Keep In Mind

Some of the commission money you make should be cycled back into your business, allowing you to pay PPC ads or to track the effectiveness of your campaigns.

If you need a little advice in getting your campaign going, consider visiting the forums where like-minded individuals (other affiliate marketers) get together. They can provide you with additional tips on how to increase your commissions.

The most important part of your affiliate marketing venture is promotion. You must always promote your product and yourself if you are going to make any commission at all. Without promotion, you can't make any money.

CHAPTER 10:
HOW TO AVOID COMPLAINTS OF SPAM AS AN AFFILIATE MARKETERS

Chapter 10: How To Avoid Complaints Of Spam As An Affiliate Marketers

People who are successful affiliate marketers have a large subscriber list that they use to market their products and ensure their business stays afloat, even in bad economic times.

However, to have this kind of list, there must be communication between the sender and the recipient. Subscribers have expectations that you'll be in constant contact with them and will address their questions and comments.

Most people know this communication will take place via email, which can also lead to spam mail.

When you become an affiliate marketer, you must do everything you can to avoid spam complaints from the subscribers. Spam is the one thing that can lead to a bad reputation for an affiliate marketer. The designation of being a spammer can even be for something trivial and keep you from being successful.

What Should You Be Mindful Of To Avoid The Spammer Designation?

The first thing you need to be mindful of is how credible your information is for your customers. Regardless of what format you send this information in – text, video or audio – it needs to be accurate and dependable. Your business will not thrive when you allow fake content to be pushed through. Your credibility will be gauged on the kind of offered content. Whatever you send to your customers, you want them to know that you are being real with them.

You want your customers to have total faith in you when it comes to the product/service you are offering just because you said it would work like you claim it would. The Internet is filled with dishonest claims and, for that reason, your target audience may not be easily enticed to buy from you. Your job as an affiliate marketer is to do your research on the product you are marketing. You don't want to be lumped in with the rest of the dishonest folks.

Test, test and retest to ensure that the product you recommend is worth the hype you're going to give it.

Your attention needs to be on the little details. Businesses will grow after some time, but only if the standards are high.

By maintaining the above standards, you won't be labeled a spammer, and your reputation won't be ruined. Your business venture will be lucrative and free of spam.

CONCLUSION

**AFFILIATE MARKETING
INFLUENCE**

Conclusion

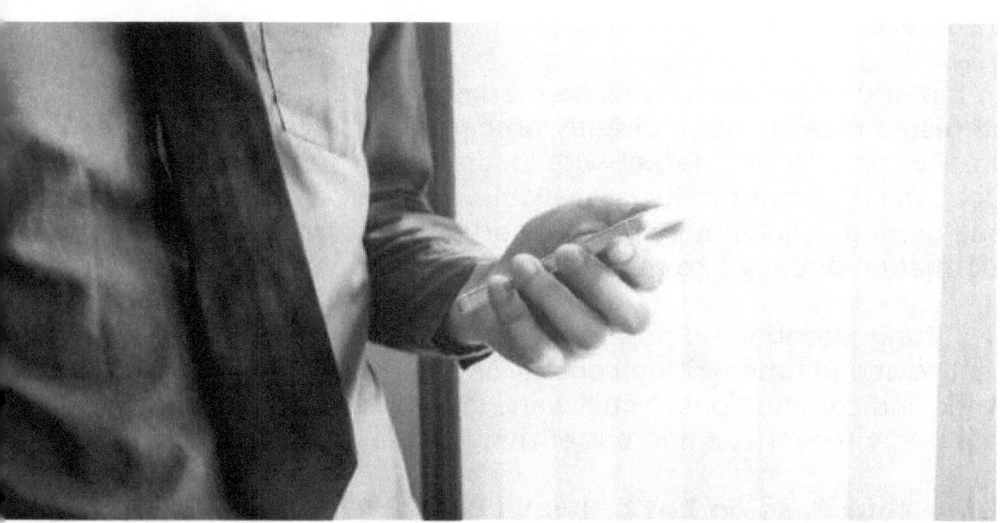

One of the best advises any person looking to become an affiliate marketer can get is to work within the confines of their passion.

This passion will help them to find products that they are personally interested in and stick with it. Niche marketing does have its place in affiliate marketing, regardless of what you may have been told.

What Are You Interested In?

Entrepreneurs are often told that when they know where their interests lie, they will have found their niche. This interest is what they are passionate about, and it allows them to sell the products better.

Don't think so?

Well, consider this: how can you sell something with real conviction if you have no passion for it? Sure, you can sell it, but you won't have the fires stimulating the flames to capture your audience's attention. Passion creates some sense of desire and urgency that spills into everything you write or say about the product.

The consensus is this: if you decide to operate in a business that you have a deep profound passion for, it's going to get noticed, and you'll automatically see sales. This sense of pride and passion will entice you to succeed.

On top of that, choosing a niche market that you feel personally interested means you're already prepared (in some sense). You already come to the market with loads of information and experience about the different products available. You don't have to spend your time getting acquainted with the market or the product. You know the information already like the back of your hand.

By putting attention on promoting products you have interest in, you'll want to spend time writing content or ads that will help garner you traffic and commissions. You'll want to blog about the product repeatedly, never running out of things to say about it.

Using Your Passion Isn't Always Best

Is there something wrong with using passion to dictate what product you promote? The answer to that is both yes and no. No, because you're bound to pay attention to what you write, come up with all kinds of ways to say something about the product and more.

However, your passion can limit you and the freedom you have to choose in products. Freedom is what you need so that you can give prospective buyers what they're looking for while you earn a commission for every product sold. A niche limits your choices, and may not be all that profitable in the grand scheme of things.

As an affiliate marketer, you want to have passion for the product you're selling, but not so much that it limits you from making good solid investments. With a little time and patience with a product you know little about, you can become passionate about it enough to write about it, to create a blog and whatever else you do to market it to your target audience.

Affiliate marketers can make really good money from their program of choice, but it comes from first doing some research and then developing material to make it happen.